The
Tafts

by
Cass R. Sandak

CRESTWOOD HOUSE
New York

Maxwell Macmillan Canada
Toronto

Maxwell Macmillan International
New York Oxford Singapore Sydney

Library of Congress Cataloging-in-Publication Data
Sandak, Cass R.
    The Tafts / by Cass R. Sandak. — 1st ed.
      p.   cm. — (First families)
    Includes bibliographical references and index.
    Summary: Examines the private life and political career of the only president to also serve as Supreme Court
justice and describes the influence of his wife, Nellie.
    ISBN 0-89686-647-5
    1. Taft, William H. (William Howard), 1857–1930—Juvenile literature. 2. Taft family—Juvenile literature.
3. Presidents—United States—Biography—Juvenile literature. 4. United States—Politics and government—1901–
1909—Juvenile literature. 5. United States—Politics and government—1909–1913—Juvenile literature. [1. Taft,
William H. (William Howard), 1857–1930. 2. Taft, Nellie Herron, 1861–1943. 3. Presidents. 4. First ladies.]
I. Title. II. Series: Sandak, Cass R. First families.
E762.S26   1993
973.91'2'092—dc20
[B]   92-37839

Photo Credits
UPI/Bettmann Archive: 4, 10, 13, 19, 27, 32, 35, 37, 40, 42, 44
The Taft Museum: 7, 9, 17, 23, 25, 29
AP—Wide World Photos: 11
Culver Pictures, Inc.: 21, 30

Macmillan Publishing Company   Maxwell Macmillan Canada, Inc.
866 Third Avenue   1200 Eglinton Avenue East
New York, NY 10022   Suite 200
                                    Don Mills, Ontario M3C 3N1

CRESTWOOD HOUSE

Macmillan Publishing Company is part of the Maxwell Communication Group of Companies.

Produced by Flying Fish Studio

Printed in the United States of America

First edition

10 9 8 7 6 5 4 3 2 1

Contents

William Howard Taft being sworn in as Chief Justice of the Supreme Court

A Dream Come True

On June 30, 1921, President Warren G. Harding appointed William Howard Taft the tenth Chief Justice of the U.S. Supreme Court. Taft was 63 years old and had waited all his life for this opportunity. Only nine years earlier, Taft had completed his term as president of the United States.

Taft served as Chief Justice until he retired from the position on February 3, 1930. This job was more important to Taft than his role as president. Becoming a Supreme Court justice had been his lifelong dream and the greatest honor that he could have received. In 1925 he wrote, "I don't remember that I ever was president."

When Theodore Roosevelt was president, he had asked Taft not once but three times to join the Supreme Court. In 1902, 1903 and again in 1906 Taft turned him down. The first two times Taft was Civil Governor of the Philippines. He felt that his work there was important and that he had the trust of the Philippine people. When Roosevelt asked him the third time, in 1906, it was obvious that Taft would probably be the Republican party nominee for president. He didn't care about being president, but Mrs. Taft did. And Mrs. Taft was a strong and forceful woman.

As Chief Justice, Taft administered the oath of office to two other American presidents, both Republican. In 1925 Calvin Coolidge was sworn in, and in 1929, Herbert Hoover. One of the justices who served on the Supreme Court at the same time as Taft was Oliver Wendell Holmes. He was one of the most distinguished figures in American history.

As Chief Justice, Taft no longer had to worry about public opinion. He would no longer be blamed for all the country's problems. In fact, Taft became what he so much wanted to be: a beloved figure in American political life. He served the office with great dignity and relish for nine years. Only old age and illness took Taft's position as Chief Justice away from him.

The Taft Family

William Howard Taft was born on September 15, 1857, in a first floor room of the Taft family house. The house was located in a well-to-do suburb of Cincinnati, Ohio, known as Mount Auburn. In the middle years of the 19th century Cincinnati was a booming town of 200,000.

Alphonso Taft, father of the future president, came from Vermont. He was the son of a farmer who had served in that state's legislature. Alphonso Taft was a lawyer who later became a judge and held many high offices. He championed the virtues of hard work, honesty and thrift, which he wanted to pass on to his young son. Alphonso was a kindly, gentle and absentminded man. From his father, Taft drew his sense of public duty.

Alphonso Taft

As a teenager Alphonso Taft was able to save enough money from teaching assignments to put himself through Yale University. He completed his college courses in 1833. Then he studied at Yale's law school.

Alphonso's marriage to Fanny Phelps ended when she died in 1852. She was just 29 when tuberculosis killed her. There were two sons, Charles and Peter, from this marriage. Alphonso Taft was 43 when he met Louisa Torrey, then 26. Eighteen months later they married, and then had their own family of three sons and a daughter.

Will Taft's mother was a New Englander, from Millbury, Massachusetts. She spent a year at Mount Holyoke, America's first women's college. She was aggressive and ambitious, thrifty and creative. When her husband was an ambassador abroad, Mrs. Taft was in charge.

Louisa's mother, and Will's grandmother, was Susan Dutton Torrey. A New Englander, she was a strong-willed and eccentric woman. When she decided to remodel her house, she simply took an axe and started knocking down the walls. She felt much of the frustration of being a woman in a man's world. Her daughters inherited this independent spirit. Until she met Alphonso Taft, it appeared that the fiercely independent Louisa would remain single.

The Taft family lived in a spacious brick house built in the Federal style. The house was large enough for a big family. There were the two boys from the first marriage plus Will and three other Taft children. Alphonso's parents also lived with the Tafts. They had moved to Ohio from Vermont when Alphonso's wife died.

As young Will grew up he had many opportunities to meet most of the country's important political figures. Alphonso Taft was appointed secretary of war by President Ulysses S. Grant in 1875. And in 1876 he also became attorney general. In 1881 President Chester Alan Arthur appointed Alphonso ambassador to Vienna, then capital of the great Austro-Hungarian empire. Later he held a similar post at the Russian court.

Louisa Taft with William. Even as a baby, Will Taft was large and his mother had trouble finding clothes for him.

William Taft, age 8

Young Taft

Young Will Taft loved baseball and played second base. He was a good player with a strong throwing arm. As a youngster he also enjoyed swimming and ice skating. A large, good-natured lad, Will was called "Big Lub" by his brothers and friends. As an adolescent he took dancing lessons. Despite his increasing size, Taft was a good dancer.

Taft graduated from Woodward High School in Cincinnati. He was second in his class. Taft enjoyed his years at Woodward so much that he returned in 1908. On the day after he was elected president of the United States, he laid a cornerstone for the new school building.

Taft spent four years at Yale University in New Haven, Connecticut. He earned his B.A. there in 1878. At Yale he also graduated second in his class. A Yale classmate remarked that Taft was "the most admired and respected man not only in my class, but in all Yale." Throughout Taft's life, his ties to Yale would remain strong. He regularly returned to the campus for Alumni Day and other events. He later taught at Yale's law school.

William Taft, when he was a student at Yale University

Two years after leaving college, Taft graduated from Cincinnati Law School. While he was still at law school, Taft supplemented his allowance from his parents. He worked as a court reporter for the *Commercial*, a Cincinnati newspaper. As a law student Taft also enjoyed Cincinnati's social life.

In May of 1880 he passed the Ohio bar exam, which allowed him to practice law. By 1881 he had been appointed to his first public office as assistant prosecuting attorney for Hamilton County, Ohio.

By this time Taft had grown to a full 6 feet 2 inches. When he graduated from college he weighed almost 250 pounds. This would increase by almost 100 pounds while he was president. He had light brown hair and blue eyes. His full handlebar mustache was a distinguishing feature.

In 1882 President Chester Alan Arthur appointed Taft a district Internal Revenue Service collector. Taft was just 24. The IRS was not to his liking, however, and he had a disagreement with President Arthur over the running of the district office. For political reasons, the president wanted Taft to replace some of his office employees. Taft refused. Within a year Taft resigned to enter private law practice.

Throughout this period Taft was active in Ohio Republican politics. After four years of private law practice, Taft was named to a judgeship on the state superior court. He was just 30. Normally it was not an appointed office, but Taft was needed to fill a vacancy. A year later he won the post by election.

Nellie Herron Taft

Nellie Herron

Born in 1861, Helen (Nellie) Herron was brought up in Cincinnati. Her well-to-do parents were Harriet Collins and John W. Herron. Mr. Herron was a lawyer who had been partners with Rutherford B. Hayes.

The Herrons sent Helen to private school where she was a devoted music student. She attended the Cincinnati College of Music. She was an accomplished musician and a serious student of languages and literature. Nor would she neglect her love of music later in life. As a young wife and mother, in 1892 she became a founder of the Cincinnati Symphony. Over the years she continued to be a patron of the orchestra.

In 1878 Nellie's parents were invited to visit President and Mrs. Rutherford Hayes in Washington. They took their 17-year-old daughter with them. Nellie was delighted by life in Washington and enthralled by the White House. She recalled later that the trip to Washington to visit the president was "the only unusual incident" in her childhood.

In 1879 Nellie met a tall law student at a sledding party. He was a few years older, but Nellie was very much taken with the man she referred to as "that adorable Will Taft."

Taft was similarly smitten with the woman he asked to be his wife. She was a petite, dark-haired, dark-eyed young woman with a bright, cheerful face. He called her a "treasure" and found her "self-contained, independent and of unusual application." They courted for five years before Nellie accepted Will's marriage proposal.

Nellie and Will were married on June 19, 1886, at the bride's parents' home in Cincinnati. Their honeymoon took them to Europe for more than three months. As a wedding gift the bride's father gave the couple a piece of land. Taft used $2,500 and money from his father to have a three-story Italianate mansion built in Cincinnati.

The Tafts had three children. They were Robert Alphonso Taft, who was born on September 8, 1889; Helen Herron Taft, born on August 1, 1891; and Charles Phelps Taft, who was born September 20, 1897.

Taft was an amiable man who was pushed by the ambition of his wife. Because in those times socially acceptable activities available to women were limited, Nellie Taft could find no satisfying outlet for her tremendous drive. She therefore had little choice but to live her life through her husband.

Taft was emotionally dependent on Nellie. Whenever they were apart he wrote at least once (sometimes several times) a day to her, detailing all his thoughts, feelings and activities. She, however, was a highly independent woman and only responded to his letters with guilt and prodding.

A Beginning in Politics

In 1890 Taft's name was given to President Benjamin Harrison as a possible candidate for the Supreme Court. Taft was just 33. Harrison felt that the young judge was not experienced enough for the Court, so he named Taft solicitor general instead. Taft served as an attorney representing the federal government before the Supreme Court. It was Taft's first taste of the inner workings of the great Court, and his work there whetted his appetite to become more closely involved with it.

The Taft family moved to Washington, D.C., where they lived for two years. Nellie was entranced with life in the nation's capital. It was during this period that Taft first made friends with Theodore Roosevelt. Roosevelt was civil service commissioner under President Harrison at the time.

Taft's father died in 1891. Taft comforted his father through his final illness. He had a deep love for the man to whom he attributed his success in life. As Alphonso Taft was dying he told his son that he believed he could be president. After Mr. Taft's death Nellie took up the cause. It had always been her goal to be married to the president of the United States.

In 1891 Taft was offered the judgeship for the Sixth Circuit. Congress had just created the federal appeals court system. The nation was divided into administrative districts. Taft's region of the Sixth Circuit covered Tennessee, Kentucky, Michigan and Ohio.

Nellie thought he should turn down the appointment. The position would take them away from Washington. She feared it would take her husband out of the mainstream of American political life and spoil his chances of becoming president.

But Taft leaped at the job. And for several years Taft was content with his role as a federal judge. Taft believed that courts "typify on earth what we shall meet hereafter in heaven under a just God." As federal judge, Taft became a champion for the rights of employees—to strike, to form unions and to receive compensation for injuries. He would later continue to fight against the abuses of big business.

Taft as a judge for the Sixth Circuit

The Philippines

Taft's career was unusual. His rise in politics came about almost exclusively through administrative appointments and not by election.

As a result of the Spanish-American War, the Philippines had recently become a U.S. possession. Owned for three centuries by the Spanish, the islands were now being administered by Americans. President William McKinley appointed Taft to the Philippines in 1899, and the next year Taft sailed to the islands.

In the Philippines Taft was at first chief civil administrator. His main job was to set up a civil government there. Taft was oppressed by the poverty he saw. The Tafts found the hot and humid climate uncomfortable and did not like the insects. At one point Taft nearly died from a bout of dengue fever, a dangerous tropical disease.

Taft did what he could to improve economic conditions in the Philippines. He oversaw the building of roads and schools. He set up courts. He extended the people's participation in their government. The intention of United States policy was to prepare the people for eventual independence and self-rule. Taft protected the interests of the Filipinos. He even went to Rome to negotiate directly with the pope over some Vatican-owned lands in the Philippines.

The Tafts lived in the Malacanang Palace, which later became the home of Philippine rulers. Mrs. Taft entered into her role wholeheartedly. She became accustomed to

Taft greets a local chieftain in the Philippines.

throwing garden parties for up to 2,000 people. She refused to segregate her guests, and so Filipinos and Americans enjoyed themselves side by side.

President Theodore Roosevelt liked Taft and kept watching the way Taft handled key situations. In 1902, while Taft was in the Philippines, Roosevelt asked him to become a member of the Supreme Court. Because Taft felt his work in the Philippines was not finished, he turned Roosevelt down. It was a sad moment, because being a Supreme Court justice was the job Taft wanted more than anything in the world. Just a few months later Roosevelt repeated the offer. Taft turned him down a second time.

Secretary of War

In 1904 Roosevelt named Taft his secretary of war. At first Taft declined, as he felt he still had work to do in the Philippines. Once Roosevelt convinced Taft that as secretary of war he could still oversee the Philippines, Taft was won over. He accepted. Since there were no wars going on, Taft had to find something else to do. He was put in charge of the U.S. Army Corps of Engineers, which was building the Panama Canal. He and Nellie visited the Canal Zone and oversaw the construction of the new canal.

As secretary of war, Taft became Roosevelt's personal adviser, especially about matters concerning foreign countries. By 1907 Roosevelt had made up his mind that Taft would succeed him as president. Roosevelt himself had lost the support of his party and was not renominated in 1908. At the Republican convention that year, Taft accepted his party's nomination.

Roosevelt and Taft were by now old friends. Once when the Tafts were visiting the Roosevelts at the White House, Roosevelt held a mock séance. He went into a fortune teller's trance. Roosevelt chanted, "I have clairvoyant powers. I see a man weighing 350 pounds. There is something hanging over his head. . . . At one time it looks like the presidency. Then again it looks like the chief judgeship." Nellie piped in, "Make it the presidency." Taft rebutted, "Make it the chief judgeship." Nellie's wish came true—first.

The 1908 Election

Taft called the presidential campaign "one of the most uncomfortable four months of my life."

Charles Taft gave speeches on his brother's behalf. He talked mainly to eastern Republicans. Meanwhile, Taft himself concentrated on wooing Roosevelt supporters. These were mainly westerners who favored Roosevelt's programs. William Jennings Bryan, running for president for the third time, was Taft's Democratic party opponent. Bryan commented that it was like running against two different candidates. One was an eastern conservative and the other was a western progressive.

A cartoon showing Theodore Roosevelt's "support" of William Taft

This split seems to show that Taft did not have a clear political philosophy. It also points up two of Taft's weaknesses: his indecision and difficulty with maintaining one position on an issue, and his desire to please everyone. The trouble was he could see everyone's viewpoint.

President Taft

Taft won the election, as was generally predicted. His most important job now was to convince Americans that he would carry on the work of Theodore Roosevelt. Taft won the election with almost the same popular vote Roosevelt had received just four years earlier.

The country was in good financial shape. There were no wars looming. Times were good. Both conservatives and progressives hailed Taft's election.

Taft's inauguration took place on March 4, 1909. As a special courtesy to his friends the Tafts, outgoing President Roosevelt had asked them to stay at the White House overnight the day before the ceremony.

The weather on Inauguration Day was stormy. Deep snow lay on the ground and freezing rain had encased the branches of trees that bowed under the weight of ice. On this wintry day Nellie Taft sat beside her husband in the carriage that took them to the ceremony at the Capitol building. No first lady had ever done that before. But Nellie felt strongly that she had earned the right to do so.

The Taft children were present as well. Because of the cold the ceremony was held indoors. Eleven-year-old Charlie brought a copy of *Treasure Island* to read during his father's speech. Mrs. Taft later reported that Charlie had never opened his book, so the speech must have been fine.

Taft was right about at least one thing. He had always joked, "It would be a cold day when I got to be president of the United States."

Nellie sits beside her husband in the carriage that will take them to the Capitol for Taft's inauguration.

The Reluctant President

Taft had become president almost against his will. As president, Taft earned the nicknames "Taft the Blunderer" and "Taft the Great Postponer." Where Roosevelt was good with the press, Taft was not. Roosevelt understood the value of public opinion and knew how to listen. Taft did not. Roosevelt was clever at promising jobs for people who supported him. Taft did not understand patronage at all.

As president, Taft seized almost any excuse to escape from the Washington routine that he disliked. He spent more time away from Washington than any earlier president.

Taft was what we would think of as a low-profile president, while Roosevelt had been a flamboyant dynamo. Americans expected the president that followed Roosevelt to be more like him, especially since Taft had been backed enthusiastically by his predecessor.

Roosevelt had also considered Charles Evans Hughes as a possible presidential candidate, but finally settled on Taft. Taft later wrote to Roosevelt, "The truth is, he [Hughes] ought to be president and then I would not have to be." Being president weighed on his spirit and transformed his personality from genial to morose.

Taft differed from Roosevelt in several significant ways. Taft did not believe in an autocratic presidency. He believed that the country should be run by its laws and not by the force of personality of a president. An admirer of Roosevelt's programs and reforms, Taft nonetheless commented that Roosevelt should have used "the legal way of reaching the same ends."

Not long after taking office Taft said to reporters, "The president has far less power than you think. He is sort of [a] figurehead for the nation for four years. He is the kind of man that they blame everything for if it goes wrong, and if it goes right he does not get any credit for it."

Among the measures of Taft's presidency was his long fight against monopolies and trusts. During his term Taft saw the break-up of twice the number of corporations that Roosevelt had targeted in his federal antitrust cases. Taft did this by using the Sherman Antitrust Act of 1890.

Roosevelt had begun a huge conservation program. But he had done it by having the government take over land to protect it. Taft managed to get Congress to approve the land acquisition, and made it legal. He also recommended levying taxes on people's incomes. He lowered import duties and fought to establish a unified, national budget.

Taft (eighth from left) at the Grand Canyon. He managed to get Congress's approval for Roosevelt's conservation program, ensuring the land's protection.

"Dollar diplomacy" became a feature of Taft's presidency. The implication was that American influence and troops—if necessary—would be used to promote America's business interests overseas. All the policy succeeded in doing was making Latin Americans, particularly, more suspicious of U.S. actions. Canada, too, became uneasy when some Americans began talking about annexation of the country.

During Taft's term in office, two states were added to the nation. In 1912 New Mexico and Arizona became the 47th and 48th states. This completed the continental United States, and it would not be until some 50 years later that Alaska and Hawaii would be added.

The 16th Amendment to the Constitution was ratified during Taft's presidency. The amendment gave Congress the right to levy a tax on people's income. Also under Taft, the 17th Amendment was drafted, although it did not become law until after he left the White House. This amendment provided for the direct election of senators.

The Taft White House

Before she became first lady, Mrs. Taft had attended Edith Roosevelt's weekly "parlor cabinets." These were get-togethers for the wives of cabinet members. They were a chance to keep abreast of what was going on in Washington. The gatherings also helped Mrs. Taft understand what was expected of her.

Mrs. Taft, pictured here in an evening gown, thoroughly enjoyed being first lady.

Mrs. Taft loved being first lady. This was in contrast to her husband, who thought the White House was "the loneliest place in the world." Mrs. Taft received visitors to the White House three afternoons a week. During those meetings she usually entertained people in the Red Room.

Mrs. Taft stationed black footmen in blue uniforms at the White House entrance. In 1909 she hired the first female White House housekeeper. The housekeeper was in charge of all food purchases and also of menus for all meals.

While the Tafts were serving in the Philippines, Mrs. Taft developed a love of Asian artifacts. The Tafts brought back many treasures from their stay in the Philippines. These included oriental screens, lacquer work and teakwood furniture. Mrs. Taft decorated the White House with many of the family's furnishings. President Taft brought many of his law books to the White House. They were symbols of his long and distinguished legal career.

The Oval Office as we know it was a creation of President Taft in 1909. Before that, the president's offices were upstairs in the family quarters. Other parts of the house were devoted to the president and his staff.

The Tafts were the first presidential family to have an automobile. Until that time all the presidents relied on horses and carriages for transportation. Overnight, the White House stables were turned into garages.

The Tafts kept cows to provide milk for the family. Their first cow was named Mooly Wooly, but she produced bad milk. So Mooly was replaced by Pauline Wayne. Kept in the White House stables until they were torn down, Pauline Wayne then wandered the lawns of both the White House

ENT TAFT AND HIS FAMILY

THEIR WHITE STEAMER

The Tafts take a drive in the first official presidential automobile.

and the nearby Old Executive Office Building. Pauline was a pet as well as a milk producer. She was much loved by the Taft family and White House staff.

Millard Fillmore was the president who first had a bathtub installed in the White House. But because Taft was such a large man, he needed an oversized tub. The special White House bathtub was installed after Taft several times had become stuck in the old narrow one. Two men were required to pull him out. There is a famous photograph showing the four workmen who installed the new tub sitting inside it.

Four workmen lounge in President Taft's bathtub.

Mrs. Taft loved gardening. She was especially pleased to have a staff of gardeners. And she could have as many roses as she wanted from the White House greenhouses, which have since been removed.

Among Washington's most famous landmarks are the beautiful Japanese cherry trees. They were planted around the city at Mrs. Taft's request. Mrs. Taft had enjoyed traveling with her husband to Japan, where she was impressed with the Japanese love of nature and beauty. Some 3,000 Japanese cherry trees were sent to Mrs. Taft as a gift from the mayor of Tokyo. Mrs. Taft planted the first two trees herself, in a ceremony on March 27, 1912. They adorn the grounds of the Capitol as well as the banks of the Tidal Basin around the Potomac River. Mrs. Taft wanted to create in Washington the atmosphere of the Luneta—a lovely park in Manila in the Philippines. The trees that help make springtime in Washington such a delight are a lasting memorial to Mrs. Taft.

The Tafts enjoyed staying outdoors on the roof of the west wing extension as much as the weather would let them. Here they could enjoy the fresh air in privacy. The Tafts also loved to relax on the White House portico. There they would listen to classical music on the newly invented phonograph. Both Tafts loved dancing, so Mrs. Taft organized a small dancing group that met regularly for fun and exercise.

Although Taft exercised every day, he hardly presented the image of a man concerned with physical fitness. His weight changed radically, and after coming to the White

House he weighed almost 350 pounds. Later in life Taft kept his weight at around 275 pounds.

Taft played golf every day and rode horseback frequently. He enjoyed motoring in the newly invented automobile. He was an avid baseball fan and relished the honorary first pitch reserved for the president to open the baseball season. Taft was the first president to take part in the national pastime; the tradition caught on and continues to the present day.

President Taft throws out the first baseball of the 1910 season. It is a tradition that continues to this day.

While they lived at the White House the Taft children—especially Charles—were interested in stories of the mansion's ghosts. There were tales that Abigail Adams haunted the East Room, that a gaunt Abraham Lincoln roamed the upstairs halls, and that an unidentified young boy with blond hair was also in residence. Taft's adviser Archibald Butt reported that Taft himself took a great interest in stories of the White House hauntings.

The Taft summer home was in Beverly, Massachusetts. The house was often called the summer White House. A closely knit family, the Tafts went there as much as possible. There Taft enjoyed sailing every evening on his boat, *The Sylph*.

Taft always liked to have people around for company, even if he was engaged in solitary activities such as reading, writing or studying papers.

For such a thoughtful and kindly man, it is surprising that while Taft was in the White House, he decided to ignore the tradition of giving gifts to the staff at Christmas. "I don't see why I should have to give them anything." And when the Tafts left the White House for good, they didn't bother to say their farewells to the staff.

The First Family

Early in 1909, only months after her husband was sworn in as president, Nellie Taft suffered a severe stroke. For a time she had difficulty speaking and moving. But her husband spent hours with her every day teaching her how to speak again.

Through her husband's love and her own indomitable will, Mrs. Taft made an almost full recovery within a year. A major triumph was her appearance at the White House New Year's reception in 1910. Guests were enchanted by her loveliness as she stood in a beautiful white crepe gown with gold embroidery. And they were also overcome by her remarkable recovery.

Later that year the Tafts' daughter, Helen, decided to leave college for a year. She wanted to experience the social life at the White House to the fullest. As the president's daughter, Helen was certainly aware that Alice Roosevelt had provoked much interest a few years earlier; Helen was probably inspired by Alice, and pushed by her mother. Helen was able to help out by being hostess during Mrs. Taft's recovery.

In December 1910, Helen's debut was the sensation of the Washington social season. Her ball was the main Christmas festivity that year. A marine band played lively tunes from an alcove above the East Room dance floor. Some 300 guests enjoyed the jolly evening. Earlier there had been a small and informal "at home" for older friends and relatives.

Mrs. Taft loved playing hostess. She remembered the evening garden party held on the White House grounds in honor of their 25th wedding anniversary in 1911 as "the greatest event" of her White House years. At this party on June 19, a crowd of approximately 4,000 invited guests swarmed across the White House lawn. The building and grounds were aglow with so many colored electric lights

A Taft family portrait. From left to right are Charles, President Taft, Helen, Robert and (seated) *Nellie.*

that the evening looked like bright daylight. Even the White House fountains sparkled with colored lights.

Charles Taft, the president's younger son, was a close friend of Theodore Roosevelt's son Quentin. Charles was thus familiar with the White House when the Taft family moved there in 1909. From the Roosevelt children he had learned to "tray slide" down the deeply carpeted marble staircase on huge trays from the White House kitchen. Even adults were known to join in the fun.

Although there were several telephones in the White House, there was just one operator handling all the calls. Charles Taft often took over when the switchboard operator went to lunch.

Older brother Robert and sister Helen also enjoyed the new home, although they were away at school during much of the time the Tafts were in the White House.

All three Taft children grew up to have distinguished careers. Robert became a famous senator from Ohio. Helen at one time was dean of Bryn Mawr, a distinguished college near Philadelphia. She was also chair of the college's history department. And Charles became a successful lawyer and mayor of Cincinnati.

Archie Butt

Taft's chief political adviser was his close friend Archibald Willingham Butt. He had been a personal aide to Taft in the Philippines. Then he served both Theodore Roosevelt and Taft during their White House years. He was a personable southern gentleman and a lifelong bachelor. He was well educated, well spoken and much in demand at Washington social gatherings. As his closest friend and confidant, he was also probably the keenest observer of Taft. His three volumes of collected correspondence give insights into Taft's mistakes and miseries.

Butt had the misfortune to be one of the passengers on board the *Titanic* when that great ship struck an iceberg and sank in 1912. When Taft was told that the ship had gone down, he ordered a ship to be sent to search for survivors. When the news came that Butt had almost certainly drowned, the president was devastated. He withdrew from the public eye for many days. As a memorial to Butt, Taft had a special fountain built in a corner of the White House gardens.

Headlines announce the tragic sinking of the Titanic. An aide and close friend to Taft, Archie Butt, drowned in the shipwreck.

A Sigh of Relief

In 1912 the Republican party renominated Taft as their presidential candidate. But Taft no longer enjoyed Theodore Roosevelt's support. This was largely because Roosevelt did not feel that Taft was decisive enough. He felt that Taft was not steering the country in the direction or manner the two had agreed upon. Taft had also upset Roosevelt by firing many of Roosevelt's appointees. Taft had hired more competent people to fill their positions.

Roosevelt thus decided to run on a third party ticket— the Bull Moose party. In this way Woodrow Wilson became the president in 1912.

An additional factor that weakened Taft's bid for the presidency in 1912 was the death of his vice presidential running mate, James Sherman. This happened just one week before the election. Sherman was an ultraconservative banker and congressman from New York who had served as vice president during Taft's first term. Even though the two had had political differences, Sherman was considered an asset on the ticket. But the dead vice president's name remained on the ballot, and voters felt they were casting a vote for a wild card, as a new vice president had not yet been named.

The Tafts had sensed in advance that Taft would lose the election. Nellie desperately wanted her husband to win, but Taft himself was more than a little relieved. Because they were fairly sure that Taft would not win, most of their belongings were packed and ready to move months before the election defeat made it necessary.

Even after the welcome if humiliating defeat of 1912, supporters suggested that Taft might again be the Republican candidate in the 1916 election. Taft responded, "I have proven…to be a burdensome leader and not one that aroused the multitude…I am entirely content to serve in the ranks."

Taft the Man

Taft had a good sense of humor about himself and his bulk. He was a great source of fun for the country. When he was secretary of war, Taft once slipped into some freshly laid asphalt on a Washington street.

Taft had a habit of falling asleep at meetings and in church. While he was asleep he snored. His wife and his adviser Archie Butt frequently saved him from embarrassment by punching him or making coughing noises. Many found Nellie a hard taskmaster and a difficult woman.

Taft always overcommitted his time. He couldn't say no. And he could not be unkind. He said, "If you have to say no, say it in such a way as to indicate to the person to whom you say it that you would like to say yes."

He made appointments with anybody who wanted to see him. He couldn't turn anyone down. As his personal aide, Archie Butt had to make excuses for Taft if he couldn't honor a commitment.

Taft overate when he felt anxious and reached his maximum weight his second year in office. Once after taking a narrow seat in a Washington theater with his

A painting of President William Howard Taft

brother Horace, Taft remarked, "Horace, if this theater burns, it has got to burn around me."

Taft was a constant traveler. He seized on any excuse to go almost anywhere for any event. He considered travel one of the duties of the president. But he shirked official duties, such as appearing before Congress and campaigning to gain support for favorite pieces of legislation.

The truth is that the presidency was a job Taft was not at all suited for temperamentally. He lacked the power of self-assertion. He was painfully afraid of offending anyone. He was therefore indecisive and put things off. He felt a continual need to apologize for himself.

Theodore Roosevelt felt that Taft did not possess "the gift of leadership. He was too easily swayed by the men around him." Roosevelt also felt Taft could not grasp progressive principles.

Taft could not bear criticism, and so comments about his abilities wounded him deeply. In 1912 he wrote, "I hope that somebody, sometime, will recognize the agony of spirit that I have undergone."

After the White House

Taft went on from the presidency to two more distinguished careers. Shortly after leaving the White House in 1913, he returned to Yale University to assume the endowed Kent professorship. As a law professor at Yale he lectured on government and international relations until 1921. In 1913 Taft was named president of the American Bar Association.

In 1921, nine years after Taft had left the White House, President Warren Harding asked him to be Chief Justice of the Supreme Court of the United States. As Chief Justice, Taft moved swiftly and helped to reduce the backlog of cases. In his nine years on the bench he wrote more than 250 decisions.

During his time as Chief Justice, Taft often walked to work in the mornings. This is remarkable considering the distance from the Taft home to the Court was about three miles. It was good exercise for a man in his sixties.

In 1914 Nellie Taft published her book, *Recollections*. The memoir contained reflections on her life as first lady. Even after the Tafts left the White House they remained active in Washington social life.

Suffering from ill health, Taft resigned as Chief Justice in early February of 1930. Just a month later, on March 8, Taft died. His body lay in state at the Capitol building. Taft's funeral service was the first funeral of a former president broadcast over radio.

Even after her husband's death Mrs. Taft stayed in Washington. She remained active and healthy, enjoying travel and classical music. Mrs. Taft died at home on May 22, 1943. She was 82 years old.

Mrs. Taft was buried beside her husband in Arlington National Cemetery in Virginia just across the Potomac from Washington, D.C. Only one other president—John F. Kennedy—is buried at Arlington.

Chief Justice William Howard Taft with his wife in his office

A painting of William Taft, president of the United States and later Chief Justice of the Supreme Court

The Taft Legacy

Taft was the only president to serve in two of the nation's highest offices: president and Supreme Court Chief Justice. He was thus head of both the executive and judicial branches of the United States government, although not at the same time.

Taft was an administrator in the tradition of certain 19th-century presidents who saw the office as that of a figurehead. The dynamic Roosevelt, serving just before Taft, and Wilson immediately after, did not fit this pattern.

Taft was also one of the few presidents who had had no congressional experience. He did not rise through the ranks of elected offices. He had been born into a well-connected political family. And he was lucky enough to have received a series of excellent political appointments that eventually took him to the highest office in the land.

Almost as soon as he became president, Taft recognized his mistake in ever accepting the office. He was not in any sense a politician. Still, he proved to be a very capable administrator.

Taft's problems were that he trusted everyone, he usually spoke his mind too freely, and he tried to please everyone. These are sterling qualities in most people, but for a president they can prove disastrous.

Roosevelt thought Taft "the most loveable personality I have ever come in contact with." James Watson, a historian and Republican congressman from Indiana, called Taft "the most likeable man ever to hold the office of president."

Throughout his life, what meant most to Taft was winning the love and approval of others, even more than pleasing himself. He was able to fulfill his family's hopes for his career. Both his father and his wife wanted him to be president, and Taft obliged them. And he eventually ended up where he himself always wanted to be—on the Supreme Court bench.

For Further Reading

Anderson, Judith Icke. *William Howard Taft: An Intimate History*. New York: W. W. Norton, 1981.

Anthony, Carl Sferrazza. *First Ladies: The Saga of the Presidents' Wives and Their Power, 1789-1961*. New York: William Morrow and Company, Inc., 1990.

Falkof, Lucille. *William H. Taft: 27th President of the United States*. Ada, Oklahoma: Garrett Educational Corporation, 1990.

Fisher, Leonard Everett. *The White House*. New York: Holiday House, 1989.

Friedel, Frank. *The Presidents of the United States of America*. Revised edition. Washington, D.C.: The White House Historical Association, 1989.

Kelly, Niall. *Presidential Pets*. New York: Abbeville Press, Publishers, 1992.

Klapthor, Margaret Brown. *The First Ladies*. Revised edition. Washington, D.C.: The White House Historical Association, 1989.

Lindsay, Rae. *The Presidents' First Ladies*. New York: Franklin Watts, 1989.

The Living White House. Revised edition. Washington, D.C.: The White House Historical Association, 1987.

Menendez, Albert J. *Christmas in the White House*. Philadelphia: The Westminster Press, 1983.

St. George, Judith. *The White House: Cornerstone of a Nation*. New York: G. P. Putnam's Sons, 1990.

Sandak, Cass R. *The White House.* New York: Franklin
Watts, 1980.

The White House. Washington, D.C.: The White House
Historical Association, 1987.

Index